# PRAYERS OF A WARRIOR


## BY


## TIM THOMPSON

## Publishers Note

Some prayers address very adult subjects and may be inappropriate for younger readers. Parents use caution.

© 2018 Pastor Tim Thompson

ISBN-13:   978-1983568862
ISBN-10:   1983568864

Cover Design - Tim Cocklin,
                    Shutterstock Images

Address all correspondence to:
timthompson74@gmail.com

# Prayers

Model Prayer ........................................................................................... 1

Prayer for the Nation ............................................................................ 2

Prayer for Help ...................................................................................... 4

Walking in Judgment ............................................................................ 5

Freedom from Curses ............................................................................ 6

Breaking Ungodly Soul Ties ................................................................ 10

Prayer for Animals ................................................................................ 13

Prayer for being sexually attracted to animals ................................. 14

Prayers for masturbating to pictures ................................................. 14

Prayer for Sex Addicts .......................................................................... 15

Prayer for Cutters .................................................................................. 15

Closing Portals ....................................................................................... 16

Prayer For Erotic Asphyxiation .......................................................... 17

Prayer for Inserting Objects ................................................................ 17

Prayer for Catholics .............................................................................. 17

Releasing Masonic Items ...................................................................... 18

Prayer for Communicating With the Dead ........................................ 18

Prayer for Seeking False Gods ............................................................. 19

Prayer for being offensive .................................................................... 20

Prayer for wanting a deeper Relationship with Jesus ...................... 20

Prayer against suicide ........................................................................... 21

Fear of man ............................................................................................. 22

Claiming to be a Christian .................................................................... 22

Breaking all Powers and Principalities .............................................. 24

Breaking the Spirit of Emotionalism .................................................. 24

Breaking the Spirit of Poverty ............................................................ 25

Breaking the Spirit of Mental Illness ................................................. 25

Binding the Spirit of Adramelech ....................................................... 26

Provisions for Finance .......................................................................... 26

Breaking Mystical Curses, Spells and Wives Tales .......................... 27

Coming Against Allah ........................................................................... 27

Fresh Anointing ..................................................................................... 28

Binding Astrology .................................................................................. 28

Breaking Atheism ................................................................................... 29

Binding Attendant Spirits ...................................................... 29
Spirit of Addiction .............................................................. 29
Breaking Speaking of Curses .................................................. 30
Breaking Channels Between Psychics etc ............................... 31
Breaking Power of Crystals ................................................... 31
Breaking the Python Spirit ................................................... 31
Breaking all Demonic Spirits ................................................ 32
Breaking Spirit of Condemnation .......................................... 32
Breaking Spirit of Oppression .............................................. 32
Spirit of Doubt .................................................................. 33
Breaking Freemasonry ......................................................... 33
Break all Secret Curses ........................................................ 35
Breaking Meditation ........................................................... 36
Feeling Abandoned............................................................. 37
Dealing with Pain .............................................................. 37
Drawing pictures of Angels................................................... 38
Worshiping Angels ............................................................. 38
Bind up the Strongman ....................................................... 38
Breaking your Bloodline ...................................................... 41
Fulfilling your Destiny ........................................................ 41
Protection ........................................................................ 42
Breaking Word and Generational Curses ................................ 43
Power Prayer ..................................................................... 44
Prayer of Protection for Your Children ................................... 45
Prayer for Finances ............................................................ 45
Your Word Becoming Flesh .................................................. 48
Prayer for Hedge of Protection .............................................48
Prayer for Help ................................................................. 49
Prayer for a Supernatural Encounter ..................................... 49
ADHD Prayer ....................................................................50
Prayer for Debt ................................................................. 51
Prayer for Pride ................................................................. 52
Directing My Steps ............................................................ 55
Breaking Generational Curses ...............................................56

**SPIRITUAL WARFARE SCRIPTURES** .................................57

# DEDICATIONS

I would like to dedicate this book to all those who don't just call themselves prayer warriors but really do actual battle for souls day and night wanting to see lives transformed and saved through the power of prayer. I would like to dedicate this book also to my dear wife for helping me and praying for me. To my dear friend, Taryn, who has blessed this ministry for several years now and has helped me beyond measure. And one more person my dear friend Dr. Dean Helland for helping me grow in the word of God.

# Model Prayer

In the name of Jesus Christ, I bind up these spirits and all spirits related to these areas. All spirits of poverty, lack, anger, depression, pride, lust, destruction, shame, disgrace, rage, perversion, bestiality, religion, unbelief, doubt, despair, suicide, control, wickedness, envy, confusion, anxiety, fear, greed, selfishness, rejection, mental illnesses, bondage, cruelty, divination, sorcery, witchcraft, spells, homosexuality, hatred, discord, jealousy, sickness, rape, incest, un-forgiveness, New Age, Satanism, occultism, murder, failure, torment, idolatry, hopelessness, frustration, foolishness, wickedness, revenge, addiction, mocking, callousness, twisting of the truth, seduction, worry, arguing, strife, suffering, illnesses, oppression, violence, manipulation, control.

Now I loose the spirit of truth, knowledge, long suffering, kindness, love, peace, joy, faithfulness, goodness, forgiveness, mercy, grace, gentleness, self-control, compassion, tongues, mercy, grace, gentleness, self-control, compassion, tongues of fire, wisdom, hope, restoration, healing, intelligence, power, self-discipline, humility, creativity, loyalty, riches, honor, strength, favor, blessing, wealth, riches, prosperity, and above all, the fear of the Lord. AMEN!

# Prayer for the Nation

Please forgive this nation for killing unborn children, for seeking the paranormal and not You. Please forgive us for getting into many wicked and perverted sexual sins. Please forgive us for looking at animals as sexual objects. Please forgive us for raping women and abusing children. Please forgive us for killing children and harming children. Please forgive this nation for turning men and woman into sex slaves. Please forgive us for throwing teenagers out on the streets as if they're trash. Please forgive us for the prostitution that is running ramped in this country.

Please loving Father, forgive us for all the ruthless and senseless killings in this country. Please forgive us for our greed and selfishness. Please forgive us for promoting violence in movies and music. Please forgive us for promoting perversion and wickedness in our music and in our movies. Please forgive us for promoting so much bestiality in movies, please forgive us for all the lust we have in our hearts. Please forgive us for not fearing You. Forgive us please for doubting You. Please forgive us for the pride we carry in our hearts. Please forgive us for the pride we have in our ministries, in our cars, in our homes, in our businesses. Please forgive us for seeking out success, power, and wealth, when all You want us to do is seek a friendship with You. Please forgive us for seeking more education and more knowledge, when we should seek You first.

Please forgive us for taking man's wisdom over Your word. Forgive us please for putting our trust in psychology over what You say. Please forgive us for seeking out Satanism, Sorcery, Magic, Mediums, Psychics, New Age, Wicca, Eastern Religions, foreign gods. Please forgive us for getting in to Erotic Asphyxiation, Sadomasochism. Please forgive us for Necrophilia. Please forgive us for wanting to speak to the dead. Please forgive us for necromancy. Please forgive us for all of our debauchery. Please forgive us for wanting to know our horoscopes. Please forgive us for allowing someone to put us under hypnosis. Please forgive us for going to a séances, listening to Tarot card readers. Please forgive us for calling white magic good. Please forgive us for glorifying the things of Satan and his demons. Please forgive us for worshiping angels. Please forgive us for putting faith in good luck charms. Please forgive us for being self-seeking. Please forgive us for our arrogance. Please forgive us for all the porn made in this country.  Please forgive us for leaving our spouses because someone is younger looking.

Please forgive us for grieving your Holy Spirit.  Please forgive us for compromising.  Please forgive us for not spending time with You.  Please forgive us for taking Your word and You for granted.  Please forgive us for the hardness of our hearts to where we mock and ridicule others especially because of their faith in You.  Please forgive us the wickedness in our prayers when actually we are speaking curses.  Please forgive us for trying to fill that void that is in our hearts that You put in there so we would have a relationship with You.  Please forgive us for turning our lives over to sex, drugs, alcohol, gambling, porn, wealth, greed, education, knowledge, power, when we should turn our lives and hearts over to You.

God the Most High God, please, please forgive us for these sins, we are a sinful nation and we need our forgiveness in this very hour. Please come dear Lord, come and bring Your glory.

Amen

# Prayer for Help

In Jesus Christ's name I bind up these spirits and all spirits connected to them.  Spirits of poverty, lack, anger, bestiality, depression, pride, lust, destruction, shame, disgrace, rage, perversion, religion, unbelief, doubt, despair, suicide, control, wickedness, envy, confusion, anxiety, fear, greed, selfishness, Rejection, mental illnesses, bondage, cruelty, divination, sorcery, witchcraft, spells, homosexuality, hatred, discord, jealousy, sickness, rape, incest, un-forgiveness, new age, Satanism, occults, murder, failing, torment, idolatry, hopelessness, frustration, foolishness, wickedness, revenge, addictions, mocking, calloused, twisting the truth, seductive, worry, arguing, strife, suffering, illnesses, oppression, violence, seducing, manipulation
Now I loose the spirit of truth, knowledge, long-suffering, kindness, love, peace, joy, faithfulness, goodness, forgiveness, mercy, grace, gentleness, self-control, compassion, tongues of fire, wisdom, hope, restoration, healing, intelligence, power, self-discipline, humility, creativity, loyalty, riches, honor, strength, great favor, blessings, wealth, riches, prosperity, and above all the fear of the Lord

# Walking in Judgment

Father in Heaven forgive me for walking in judgment towards others, I have been more concerned about someone smoking cigarettes or smelling like cigarettes than I have been about showing the love of Jesus Christ. I have been acting like the Pharisees; it's not a matter of what goes in a body but what is in the heart of man. I should be more concerned about walking in the power, love, gentleness, authority and compassion of You, Father, than be concerned about a person smoking.

Father in Heaven, please forgive me for being legalistic and judging companies that promote lingerie, who am I to judge a person or a company? There is not one scripture in the bible that says lingerie is evil but yet I stand in judgment because I don't like that clothing, but when did I become so powerful and so self-righteous that I could speak against something. If I don't like something I should be praying for it and not cursing it.

Father in Heaven, please forgive me for standing in judgment and mocking Christian rock music, please forgive me for speaking against another child of yours anointing, who am I to claim what is or isn't from you? If you called one man to scream or talk softly in music it is none of my business and you didn't ask me for my opinion.

# Freedom from Curses

Now that we realize there are curses, we need to realize why there are curses and what the effects of curses are.

#1 Reason for a curse is not listening to what God says; when God speaks we need to listen. If you want the blessings of God do what He says to do.

#2 So many people say, well, I don't know what God is saying, if you're a spirit filled Christian you should be able to determine what God is wanting or asking you to do. See, sometimes we get off track but when we do God is quick to help us if we walk in humility and love.

If God is so powerful to create the world and us, do we really believe that he would keep his will for our lives a secret? Each child of God, God has a plan and a purpose for our lives. God almighty loves us so much that He wants us to be filled with joy and peace but we must humble ourselves and seek His face to find out what it is that He's calling us to do. Many times what we want is what God has put in our hearts to do in life for His glory not ours.

Now read this carefully: By being obedient to God here's the list of blessings listed in Deuteronomy, Chapter 28. As you read this list please think about these blessings.

1. Exaltation

2. Reproductive

3. Health

4. Prosperity

5. Victory

6. That we are the head and not the tail

7. That we will be above and not beneath.

Now that we can see clearly what the blessings are let's now look at the curses.

A. Humiliation

B. Barrenness

C. Sickness and disease of every kind

D. Poverty, failure, lack

E. Defeat in every area of life.

F. We will be the tail and not the head

G. We will be below and not above

H. Confusion

# Indications of Curses:

(1) Mental, emotional, financial and spiritual breakdown

(2) Repeated sickness or diseases, especially hereditary sickness.

(3) Feminine problems - barrenness, miscarriage, menstruation problems or uncommon bleeding.

(4) Breakdown of marriage, breakdown in relationships, siblings fighting as adults, family alienation, and lack of mercy or love between children.

(5) Financial insufficiency, poverty, lack, car accidents repeated, loss of jobs over and over again, or getting hurt on the job at several different jobs, Accident prone.

(6) People dying at early ages or unexplained deaths.

There are also generational curses.

I have seen a location be under a curse to where no matter what the business is it either went under or evil things have happened at this location. It's very sad but this one place that was just a small bar off the highway had more deaths and rapes than big bars or night clubs. When a place has had a violent, evil or wicked crime committed on its land that land must be prayed over or that location belongs to demonic powers.

One time a man bought a car that a person had committed suicide in and after he took ownership of that car he then felt suicidal thoughts and he finally came to a point where he got rid of the car, then all the thoughts of suicide left him.

We need to realize we live in a nonstop spiritual war. Now here are some reasons that we come under a curse.

A. Having false gods, are you putting your trust in an Ouija board, Tarot cards, dreams, crystals, good luck charms, sex, alcohol, drugs, gambling, séances, wizards, dream catchers, horoscopes, or mediums or witches? If you are then you have put a curse on yourself and your family because God the creator of heaven and earth must be on the throne at all times. How can we say we love God but we don't trust him? (Exodus 20: 3& 4, Deuteronomy 27: 15)

B. Disrespect for parents, so many young people these days are killing and harming their parents and then wonder why they are being locked up for many years. Young people I realize that life isn't easy but remember if you commit a crime you eventually will do the time. So many young people will never have a family and will never experience the joys of life because they are sitting behind bars just waiting for their life to end because every day that they wake up they will sit behind prison or mental ward walls. (Deuteronomy 27: 16)

C. Treachery against a neighbor, who is your neighbor? A friend, a church member, a co-worker, see, we must represent Christ at all times. Anyone that comes to you is your neighbor. Deuteronomy 27: 17)

D. Injustice to the weak, if you study your word you will find throughout scriptures that God has a heart for those that are poor and those that are fatherless. (Deuteronomy 27: 18 & 19)

E. Illicit sex Deuteronomy 27: 20-23, and Revelation 9:21 "And they did not repent of their murders or their sorcerers or their sexual immorality or their thefts". See, if you have sex with an animal, or person outside of a man and woman marriage, you are in sin. So many times people think that I only had oral sex with this person or with this animal so that can't be wrong but in the eyes of God it is wrong.

Now here is a list of why so many fall under a curse:

Stealing, lying, being cruel to animals or children, having no mercy, showing lack of love or compassion, self-seeking or self-centered, prideful, boastful, angry, easily angered, murder, rape, incest, doing evil against God's anointed, harming or being destructive towards your neighbor's things or harming or being destructive towards the house of God, harming or being destructive towards a poor person, speaking evil against someone that is seeking after the heart of God, name calling, names to a person that is a Christian, being self-righteous, husbands not forgiving their wives, husbands not honoring and respecting their wives with their words and actions, husbands that treat their wives poorly, husbands that compare their wife's body to what they saw in a porn magazine or movie, husbands that look at porn or get into calling 1-800 # to talk to another woman in a lustful conversation, Wives that dishonor their husbands because they are speaking evil about them. Wives that withhold sexual gratification from their husbands because he doesn't make enough money for you to be happy, or buy you enough things. Men that treat their wives like a sex toy.

# Breaking Ungodly Soul Ties

## *Two more reasons for a curse to come upon you:*

**A. Objects in homes (Deuteronomy 7: 26)** We are to have no abominable things in our home. Years ago I was given a beautiful necklace and it had a nice stone with it. Well I went to go get it cleaned and the jeweler who I knew was a Christian said, "Tim, you have got to see this", well he showed me the nice stone under a magnifying glass and it was a Buddha Temple inside the stone. Well we destroyed both the necklace and the stone because anything connected to Buddha, which is a false god, a Christian should have nothing to do with.

Then also years ago a woman came to me and said my children suffer from severe nightmares but my husband and I don't know why. Well I knew this couple were Christians and they stood against Disney so I could not think of what would cause their children to have nightmares. So I went over to their house and someone had given this little child of theirs Pokémon cards, so I explained to them that Pokémon means **"monster in your pocket"**, so I asked the little one, do you want your nightmares to go away? Well he said yes, so I said can we burn all these cards? And he said yes, so we did and that little boy no longer had nightmares. See Satan will not knock on your door asking to come in, he will find a way to destroy you and your family if he can.

B. **Soul ties; these are soul ties which are contrary to God's purposes**, In adultery, fornication (especially past sexual relationships). Ungodly soul ties can bring spiritual sickness. I tell people anything related to that past ungodly soul tie relationship needs to be destroyed, stuffed animals, jewellery, clothes, etc, anything that causes you to look back like Lot's wife did before she became a pillar of salt because she looked back at Sodom and Gomorrah before God destroyed it.

**1 Corinthians 6: 18: Flee sexual immorality**. "Every sin that a man does is outside the body, but he who commits sexual immorality sins against his own body". See, oaths are not of God but many people have cut themselves and taken an oath, we need to repent from all oaths and ungodly soul ties. My graduating class was so evil and self-centered that I have decided not to have any contact with my old classmates because hardly any of them see any of the wrongs that we did. Can light fellowship with darkness?'

Ok, it's time to break these curses, so let's look at these scriptures closely:

**1 John 3:8** "He who sins is of the devil, for the devil has sinned from the beginning. For this purpose the Son of God was manifested, that He might destroy the works of the devil.

**Isaiah 10:27** "It shall come to pass in that day That his burden will be taken away from your shoulder, And his yoke from your neck, And the yoke will be destroyed because of the anointing oil. We must repent from all sin".

A. We must renounce in the name of Jesus Christ, all demonic activity and sinful activity of our past and/or our parent's or grandparent's past. We must repent and ask God to forgive and sever all demonic curses, soul ties, and actions related to that curse.

B. We must resist the evil one and submit under God. James 4: 7:" Therefore submit to God. Resist the devil and he will flee from you". The devil is a liar, so if he says you're going to be worthless just like your mom was or your dad was tell him you're a liar. Just because your aunt and mom were prostitutes doesn't mean you have to be. Or just because your father is in prison doesn't mean you have to go there as well.

C. Now meditate on the word of God believe it, memorize it, stand on it and confess what you want God to do in your life by speaking out scriptures. God loves you and He truly does have a plan and a purpose for your life so please draw close to Him and He will draw close to you.

# Now here are just a few examples of how to break curses:

In Jesus Christ's name, I ask you Heavenly Father to forgive my grandfather for being a mason and I ask that all demonic curses and oaths that were spoken out will be broken as of right now in the name of Jesus

Christ and through the blood of Christ I have been redeemed from all demonic curses and powers. So as of this second I am now free in Christ.

If your parents called you names here's one just for you;

In the name of Jesus Christ I am free from all demonic and evil word curses that my parents spoke over me because according to the word of God I am more than a conquer through Christ Jesus, So now I sever all demonic curses spoken over me and I plead the blood of Christ over me spiritually, mentally, financially, emotionally and my whole being.

If you give God more of your time, love and energy you will find out none of it was in vain. God will reward those that seek His face.

I don't know if anyone has heard of the movie (Facing The Giants) but I would like to strongly recommend that you watch this movie because it will change your life, because it has brought many blessings to me.

So many don't realize that Jesus Christ not only wants to help you discover your destiny but help you to reach your destiny in life. So many people have got so many wrong concepts about Jesus Christ because so many people have been hurt by them, abused them, tore them down, and betrayed them. But I am here to tell you no matter what sin or wrong you have done in life God wants to forgive you.

**John 3:16** "for God so loved the world that He gave His only begotten Son, that whoever believes in Him should not perish but have everlasting life".

So please cry out to Jesus Christ right now and just say "Jesus, forgive me for my sins and come inside of me and be my Lord and Savior. Teach me Your ways and Your concepts and Your decrees. Now I ask this in Jesus Christ's Holy name. Amen.

# Prayer for Animals

Father in Heaven, I ask that You will please forgive me for being sadistic towards animals, people or my spouse. I am so deeply sorry for being sexually aroused, by wanting to harm someone or something. Please Father, by your mercy and grace, I ask that You will teach me how to love someone, animals or my spouse with a holy love and a genuine love.

Please Father in Heaven teach me how to be gentle hearted and teach me how to be pure, give me a heart of flesh.

Please Father in Heaven, uproot all the seeds of cruelty, wickedness, vengeance, and evil out of my heart and I humbly ask You, please will You give me a heart of mercy, compassion, grace, love, kindness and understanding.

Please Father forgive me for having a desire to want to kill myself or someone else. Give me Your heart and please teach me to be like Christ.

Father in Heaven, please forgive me for having sex with animals anal or oral, I know it is wrong so please wash

my mind and my whole being in the blood of Jesus Christ. Father please take away the desires I have of wanting to have sex with animals and please give me a heart of purity and holiness. I am so sorry my Father for seeing animals as sex objects, wash my mind and teach me how to be pure and Holy, in Jesus Christ's name I ask these prayers and I seal these prayers in the blood of Jesus Christ. Amen.

Please Father in Heaven; forgive me for being sadistic and cruel to animals or people, even to children. I am so sorry that I have abused the power I have and the strength over people. Please Lord Jesus Christ teach me how to walk in humility, compassion and love. Forgive me Father for my ignorance, pride, selfishness and ego. Please come now Lord Jesus and help me become more like You, In Jesus Christ's name I pray. Amen

# Prayer for being sexually attracted to animals

Father in Heaven please forgive me for being sexually attracted to animal furs, I am so sorry that I become sexually aroused when looking at dead animals or the furs of animals. Please uproot any sick and perverted sexual thoughts or ideas in me and uproot them. In Jesus Christ's name I ask You will help me become a man of God and I ask in Jesus Christ's name to give me a heart of purity, in Jesus Christ's name. Amen.

# Prayers for masturbating to pictures

Father in Heaven please forgive me for masturbating to pictures of dead men or women and even animals. I am so deeply sorry that I become sexually aroused by pictures of dead men or women who have been killed in an accident or been beaten to death.

Please Father help me discover what is pure and Holy and give me desires that are from You that are pure and righteous.

Please Father in Heaven uproot the evil and wicked seeds planted in me and give me a heart of God. Lord Jesus Christ please give me the heart of Christ and please show me what Your desires are and teach me what it means to have healthy and normal sexual desires according to Your word. In Jesus Christ's name I ask that You cleanse my mind of all evil in Jesus' name. Amen.

Father in Heaven please forgive me for wanting to sexually touch several women that I have seen pictures of in the newspaper or on the news that have been beaten to death, took their own lives or have been killed in an accident.

I am so deeply sorry Father that I wanted to have sex with so many of these women or take one of their hands and masturbate with it. Father in heaven I need your help I have had so many evil and wicked desires please come and rescue me, I am consumed in thoughts of evil perversion and thoughts of sexual evil thoughts, help me, I am crying out loud, please. I surrender all to you, help me Lord Jesus.

In Jesus Christ's name I ask that my mind and whole entire being be washed and cleansed in the blood of the lamb. Amen. And now I seal these prayers in Jesus Christ name. Amen

# Prayer for Sex Addicts

Father in Heaven please forgive me for being a sex addict and looking at the opposite sex as a piece of meat. Please forgive me for not honoring and respecting others as my brothers and sisters in the Lord. Please forgive me for wanting to have sex hourly and thinking about having sex with everyone I meet and forgive me for lusting in my heart non-stop after so many. Please Loving Father give me the heart of Christ Jesus and teach me how to walk in purity and holiness. Please wash my mind of lust and give me pure and holy eyes in Jesus Christ's name I pray. Amen

# Prayer for Cutters

Father in Heaven please forgive me for cutting myself, burning myself and harming myself. I am so deeply sorry for looking at myself and comparing myself to a maggot or a piece of trash. Lord Jesus You suffered for me and You were crucified for me, I am so sorry I have discovered no human value in myself and I am so sorry I have found no value of any part of me. I am so sorry that instead of turning to You for comfort I have turned to cutting and punishing myself for so many reasons. Please Lord Jesus restore my mind, my heart and my emotions and please Lord Jesus teach me how to walk hand in hand with you hourly, in Jesus Christ's name I pray. Amen.

# Closing Portals

Several people have sent me messages or made comments, how do I close a portal? Please listen carefully, no matter what you have done repent, yes repentance is the first part of being set free. See God is looking for humility, look at this scripture, when we humble ourselves the power of God moves.

Acts 19:19 Also, many of those who had practiced magic brought their books together and burned *them* in the sight of all. And they counted up the value of them, and *it* totaled fifty thousand *pieces* of silver.

If you were given anything by the other person that you were in sin or unholy relationship with, such as rings, flowers, cards, bras, lingerie, sex toys, stuffed animals, whips, chains of any kind, Tarot cards, Ouija board, crystals, dream catcher, pictures, etc, I would strongly suggest you destroy them to where nobody can have them or would want them but if you can't destroy it bury it deep in the ground! Such things symbolize the ungodly relationship and can hold a soul tie in place.

I have met people who had a close grandma leave her Ouija board to her granddaughter and all of a sudden this woman's life was being destroyed because of the demonic power coming off of this board.

I have also met a young man who was left original pictures of several serial killers and he started developing mental problems. See, God wants to bless you, question is are you willing to humble yourself to be set free?

God has called you to walk in victory, joy and peace but so many want to try to either put a band aid on the situation or want to think there's another way so they turn to psychology, new age, medicine man, witchdoctor, a Catholic priest, some sort of eastern religion, but there's nothing that can set you totally free except the power of Jesus Christ, so please humble yourself today right now and just say "Lord Jesus Christ forgive me for my sins and cleanse me with Your blood please. I ask right now that You would sever all ties with demonic powers from them to me or me to them. In Jesus Christ's name I plead the blood over these prayers. Amen.

# Prayer For Erotic Asphyxiation

Father in Heaven forgive me for harming myself or hurting myself by trying Erotic asphyxiation. Please forgive me for strangling myself and not realizing my life isn't based on getting sexual fulfillment but my life is based on serving You. Please help me get sexual fulfillment by making love to my spouse and not through other means. In Jesus Christ's name I pray. Amen.

# Prayer for Inserting Objects

Father in Heaven please forgive me for putting objects up myself or in me to become sexually pleased. I am asking You to please help me to become sexually pleased by my spouse whom I am married to. Please give me a heart for my spouse and not a toy or object to help me get sexually off in Jesus Christ's name I pray. Amen

# Prayer for Catholics

Father in Heaven please forgive me for holding onto my grandmother's rosary beads and anything else that I knew was from the enemy. I am so sorry I allowed my emotions to be over taken to where instead of standing up for the things of God, I allowed Satan to convince me that I needed to keep things because of sentimental value. Lord Jesus Christ forgive me please and please You be my Lord, not my emotions. Amen

Father in Heaven forgive me for keeping my grandparent's statues of Mary and of Jesus that came from a Catholic church. I am so sorry that my thoughts and emotions were more wrapped up in sentimental values instead of destroying something that I know was an idol and is just looked

at as a piece of religion and nothing to do with a deep and meaningful relationship. So in Jesus Christ's name please forgive me and help me destroy all religious items.

## Releasing Masonic Items

Father in Heaven please forgive me for holding onto any of my grandfather's masonic items or holding onto any of my grandfather's or dads items that they got when they were in the war that have a Buddha or a Swastika on them. All items that have wicked and evil symbols on them need to be destroyed no matter how much they claim it is worth, it is still under a curse and in the eyes of God it is evil to have in your home. So please dear God forgive me for keeping these things and now give me the strength to bury them. Amen.

# Prayer for Communicating With the Dead

Father in Heaven please forgive me for trying to communicate with my dead dad, mom, sister, brother, grandparent, cousin, friend or any other person. I am so deeply sorry for trying to communicate with the dead thinking it was ok for me to do this. I am so sorry for trying to get advice from a dead relative, bible hero, or a dead world leader. God Almighty my trust and my desires should be in You and You only. Forgive me for trying to gain financial, spiritual or some wisdom from the dead by gaining insight from the other side. Father in heaven please help me to seek Your face, give me a desire and a heart to know you. In Jesus Chris's name I pray. Amen

Father in Heaven please forgive me for seeking wisdom, insight, my healing, prosperity or blessings by putting my trust in my Horoscope, yoga, séances, Tarot cards, Ouija board, psychic, medium, palm reading, body reading, star gazing, water wishing, tea leaves, voodoo, angel worship, demon worship, fire gazing, chanting, hypnosis, good luck charms, crystal ball, my pastor, my friend, my mom or my dad, auto writing, wearing certain clothes, throwing salt over my shoulder, crucifix or by holding a rosary. My God, My God forgive me for not humbling myself and putting my trust in the one and only true way to find answers to life and that is Jesus Christ. Please Lord Jesus Christ, forgive me for being so stubborn and prideful by not seeking Your face and seeking the true heart of God. Lord Jesus Christ; restore my life and help me stay on the right path walking with You, Lord Jesus Christ hourly. Amen.

# Prayer for Seeking False Gods

Father in Heaven, please forgive me for falling away from You and seeking after false gods. Forgive me please for allowing sin and the pleasures of sin to draw me away from You and not realizing I was falling into a deeper deception, thinking the pleasures of sin would last forever but I was deceived and now I am hurting and lost. Please, Lord Jesus Christ I plead with You, restore me please to where I can feel the heart of God leading and guiding me into your truth and your ways. So in Jesus Christ's name give me a new hope and a deeper than before relationship with You Jesus, please, and help me restore my faith in You, in Jesus Christ's name I pray. Amen.

## Prayer for being offensive

Father in Heaven forgive me for holding an offense towards those that have used me and have hurt me, God may You bless those that have cursed me, used me and have hurt me. Lord Jesus when they were crucifying you, You said, "Lord, forgive them for they know not what they are doing", so I ask you Jesus Christ give me a heart like Yours and give me a compassion to love people like You do. Lord Jesus Christ give me a heart to know the deep intimacy love of God and help me walk in the deepness of love daily towards people. Now I ask these prayers to be sealed in the blood of Christ. Amen.

## Prayer for wanting a deeper Relationship with Jesus

Father in heaven I want to be deeper in a relationship with you, I want to know if I hurt You or offend You, so please I am crying out, Lord Jesus if there is anyone or anything in my life that puts a wall or a blockage from me being in a deeper relationship with You then please show me and give me the strength to remove it please. Lord Jesus my heart just breaks because I want to know You and I want to hear You. Please give me a deeper desire to want to know You and fall deeper in love with You. My life and heart are in Your hands, please draw me closer Lord Jesus Christ and let me experience so much more of You and let me feel Your presence. Lord Jesus be tangible, consume me in Your love, my Lord and Savior. Lord Jesus let me just be in awe of You daily. Breathe on me Jesus Christ to where I can feel it and shout for joy because I know it's You. Lord Jesus I want You, yes I want so much more of You. Consume me Lord Jesus Christ and I ask these prayers in Your awesome name in Jesus Christ. Amen.

Lord Jesus Christ please forgive me for not casting down thoughts and imaginations. Lord Jesus I know it is sinful to think about having sex with the same sex, please forgive me for entertaining thoughts of wanting to kiss someone of the same sex as me and forgive me for claiming it's just for fun when I know Jesus Christ died on a cross because of sin, so sin must never be referred to as just for fun. Please Lord Jesus Christ forgive me for not taking heed to what Your word says. Please give me a heart of flesh and a heart that would take heed to Your word. In Jesus Christ name I pray. Amen.

# Prayer against suicide

Lord Jesus Christ forgive me for entertaining thoughts of suicide. I am deeply sorry Lord Jesus for not casting these thoughts and imaginations down. You created me for a purpose so it is not right that I would entertain evil thoughts when I know that You made me and Your only Begotten Son, Lord Jesus, died on a cross so there is hope even when I can't see it. Please Father in Heaven forgive me for listening to spirits telling me there is no hope and life is meaningless.

**(Please if you are feeling suicidal contact a pastor right away or a professional please)**

Father in Heaven please forgive me for believing in lies about love because love is not being controlled, called filthy names, love is not slapped, cussed at, spit on, punched, kicked, laughed at, made fun of, ridiculed, beat on, have your hair pulled out, being degraded, being made to feel worthless, being forced to have sex, being raped, being burned, being forced to sleep in a dog pen, being forced to sleep in a garage, being withheld food, sleep, clothes, being forced to surrender all your money or your worldly possessions, feeling threatened, being manipulated, being lied to, being used, being forced to eat dog or cat food, being cut, being knifed, burned, tortured, being forced to suffer, being forced to wear a dog chain or dog collar, being sodomized, being drugged, forced to lose weight, threatened, being forced to do anything that is mentally, emotionally, psychical or spiritual that is harmful to you or life threatening. Being forced to do anything that you feel is mentally, emotionally, spiritually or psychically wrong. Also love is not being a punching bag for anyone. Being told you need to lose weight or you need to change the clothes you wear, or the way you are, and love is not staying with a spouse that cheats on you with other women or men.

1 CORINTHIANS 13:4-7 tells us what love is,

4 Love suffers long and is kind; love does not envy; love does not parade itself, is not puffed up;

5. does not behave rudely, does not seek its own, is not provoked, thinks no evil;

6. does not rejoice in iniquity, but rejoices in the truth;

7 bears all things, believes all things, hopes all things, endures all things.

Father forgive me for not humbling myself and sexually satisfying my partner, I know in part it is my fault that they have fallen into sin because I didn't desire to have sex for so long I set up my spouse to fall. Please give me a heart to love my spouse sexually, mentally, emotionally and help me to find my spouse attractive even though they have gained weight. Father in Heaven forgive me for not being there to listen to their needs and their desires. I am so sorry I ignored my spouse when they needed to talk and just share their heart. I am so sorry dear God when my spouse needed just to have a shoulder to cry on or someone to just open up to or just a soft word of encouragement I wasn't there emotionally for them.

When my spouse needed to be honored and stood up for I allowed my family to tear my spouse down because I was a coward and was walking in fear of man. Please Lord Jesus forgive me for claiming to be a Christian but denying the power of God living in me by being a coward, I am deeply ashamed of myself and I ask you please Lord Jesus forgive me and help me become that person in You that will walk in the power and authority in Christ Jesus I pray now and seal these prayers in Your blood. Amen.

# Fear of man

Father in Heaven please forgive me for denying Your power and walking in fear of man. I know You asked me to do this or that but Lord Jesus because of the fear of man or offending my parents, siblings or friends I didn't do what You really showed me what You wanted me to do because of fear and because I have been a coward. Please Lord Jesus give me a heart to know Your will and Your ways and now help me to walk in the power and authority in You Lord Jesus Christ.

Help me Lord Jesus Christ not to be a coward and walk in fear and rebellion. Lord Jesus forgive me, I am so deeply sorry for not being that powerful person in You and doing what I know I was called to do. So in Jesus Christ's name be strong where I am weak in Christ Jesus. Amen.

# Claiming to be a Christian

Father in Heaven I am so deeply sorry I claim to be a Christian and I claim to love You but I am doing what Jesus rebuked people for doing, he said, "Why do you call me Lord, Lord but not do what I tell you to do". Father I am so phony because I claim to love Jesus so much but I don't do any of the things He has told us to do, forgive me for worrying about offending someone and forgive me for being a coward.

Lord Jesus I know You are shaking the fence and I must decide whose side will I stand for, the power of God or the power of Satan, you didn't call me Lord Jesus to be lukewarm. How can I claim to love You, Lord Jesus but not do what You say to do?

Father in heaven help me to follow the words of Jesus Christ and help me become not just a hearer of the word of God but an actual doer of the word of God. Father in Heaven please don't have Your son puke me out of His mouth, give me a heart that will catch on fire for the things of God and help me to learn how to walk in the things of Jesus. In Jesus Christ's name I ask that my heart would be transformed to be like Jesus Christ. Amen

Father in Heaven please teach me how to walk in faithfulness, accountability, teachable, power, authority, humility and above all things love. Please give me a heart to want to give a dying world that is filled with sin that there is hope in Jesus Christ. Amen

# Breaking all Powers and Principalities

In Jesus Christ's name I come against principalities, against powers, against the rulers of the darkness of this age, against spiritual hosts of wickedness in the heavenly places, and I bind you up right now in Jesus Christ's name to where you cannot and will not operate at all. All your plans and all your tactics have been crushed now, I openly expose you to

the light and from this day forward this house, room, business, property, land is now under the power and authority of the living Jesus Christ who is Lord and Savior of all, so by His blood this place has now been set free

Where there is freedom there is the Spirit of the most high God who raised Jesus Christ from the dead, so Praise Jesus Christ, it's time to get excited.

# Breaking the Spirit of Emotionalism

In Jesus Christ's name I come against the spirit or emotionalism, I refuse to allow my emotions to control me and be a god to me, Jesus Christ is my Lord and Savior and even though I may deeply desire to live near a friend or family member, or I may desire to keep this or that because it is an antique, like my dad giving me a porn magazine from the 60s, or my mom giving me a rosary from the 40s, no matter how much it is worth I will destroy it because no matter what it is or how much my heart longs for it I want nothing to come in between my relationship with Jesus Christ, so right now I demand my emotions and my heart's desires to come under submission of the power of God and I want the heart of God in me, so in Jesus Christ's name, I declare Jesus Christ is Lord over my emotions and wants, in Christ Jesus I pray. Amen

# Breaking the Spirit of Poverty

In Jesus Christ's name I come against the spirit of lack and poverty, you have no right being in my life, my spouse's life or my child's life, I come against you, not in my name or in the power I have but in the name of Jesus Christ and in the power and authority of Jesus Christ's name I come against you. I break your power and I crush your power in Jesus Christ's name and I now release the anointing of God to bless me with every blessing and needs I have and I ask that if any demon that tries to stop the flow of my blessings and prosperity will be severely punished and sent back where it came from. In Jesus Christ's name I ask these things.

In Jesus Christ's name seal in the anointing, power, authority and power in Christ's name. Amen.

# Breaking the Spirit of Mental Illness

In Jesus Christ's name I come against the spirit of mental illness and I declare from this day forward that the spirit of fear will not cause mental illness in me, my spouse or child anymore, for God Almighty has not given me or my spouse or my child a spirit of fear but of power love and a ( sound mind ) since so many mental illnesses come from fear, and so many take their life because they fear this or that I come against this spirit and I declare that wherever I go I pray that peace, power, authority, love and a sound mind will be released through the power of the Holy Spirit living in me, now I speak these things out and ask Jesus Christ to anoint and bless my prayers in Jesus Christ's name and sealed in the name of Jesus Christ, covered in the Blood. Amen.

# Isaiah 54 v 17

In Jesus Christ's name, right now I declare that no word, nor weapon formed, planned and spoken against me shall prosper in any way shape or form. I declare that Jesus Christ's name is above every name and above every curse so whatever anyone says or thinks of me I cast all things down under the blood of Jesus Christ's name and I pray right now that my shield of faith is mighty and stopping the arrows from the enemy. I pray that Jesus, yes Jesus Christ my friend, my Savior, my Lord and Light will protect me and lead me into a deeper walk with Him and the loving Holy Spirit will lead me and guide me into all truth and the knowledge and wisdom of truth Amen. I pray in Jesus Christ's name. Amen.

# Binding the Spirit of Adramelech

In Jesus Christ's name I bind up the spirit of Adramelech which deceives women into believing that having sex with animals would be ok and sexually satisfying. I bind up this spirit and all perverted spirits with it and I send you back to where you came from, you no longer will hold any power or authority in my neighborhood or city in Jesus Christ's name I prayer. Amen. And I ask Lord Jesus Christ that You will protect me from all demonic powers. In Jesus Christ's name. Amen

# Provisions for Finance

In Jesus Christ's name, I ask that You, Lord Jesus Christ, will spiritually, mentally, emotionally physically and financially bless and protect me. Dear Lord Jesus Christ please help me and break every curse that has ever been spoken over me. Now I ask you Lord Jesus Christ to bless me as I am calling in blessings from the North, South, East, and west in Jesus Christ's name I pray. Amen.

Father in Heaven I ask in Jesus Christ's name that the spirit of Adrammelech, which is the spirit that drives people to commit human sacrifices, is bound up and it will not be allowed to operate anywhere near my home that I live in or the city or town I live in. Please Father, in Jesus Christ's name, send this spirit back to where it came from and In Jesus Christ's name I pray that this spirit will not be able to operate in any way near where I live. In Jesus Christ's name. Amen

# Breaking Mystical Curses, Spells and Wives Tales

In Jesus Christ's name I come against all mystical curses, spells or wives tales; curses you have no power or authority to be near me or come against me. I send you back right to where you come from and in Jesus Christ's name I ask in Jesus Christ's name the power you have and hold on to will be broken, destroyed and crushed in Jesus Christ's name I pray. Amen.

Now I ask Father that you will bless me and bring forth mighty blessings in my life because of evil being spoken against me in Jesus Christ's name amen.

# Coming Against Allah

In Jesus Christ's name I come against the false god called Allah which is the god of the Muslim religion. I ask Lord Jesus Christ that this false god and evil religion will not be able to advance any further and you would bind up these false teaching and beliefs. Please Lord Jesus Christ open up the hearts and minds of these people and show them, Lord Jesus Christ, Your awesomeness and reveal to them just how much You love them, in Jesus Christ's name I pray. Amen.

In Jesus Christ's name I bind up all Familiar spirits, Ancestral spirits, and Generation spirits, you are no longer allowed to operate around me and I come against you in the name of Jesus Christ. I come against all your demonic plans and I come against all your demonic insights. In Jesus Christ's name you no longer will be able to operate or gain any type of insight about me because I am covered by the blood of Jesus Christ and in Jesus Christ's name I was bought by the blood of the lamb. Now I ask Lord Jesus Christ to push back the enemy and have mighty blesses be poured out on me in Jesus name. Amen.

# Fresh Anointing

In Jesus Christ's name, I ask Lord Jesus Christ to please release a fresh new anointing and let there be a whole new level of Apostolic warfare released in my church and in the churches surrounding this area I live in, plus release this powerful anointing in Churches, for example Churches in Dallas, Texas or Seattle, Washington. Now Lord Jesus Christ raise up your children to walk in this powerful anointing and help them to continue to walk in humility. In Jesus Christ's name I ask that these things be done according to your perfect will, in Jesus Christ's name. Amen.

# Binding Astrology

In Jesus Christ's name I bind up the demonic powers of Astrology and I ask, You, Lord Jesus Christ that these people would be deeply convicted of their sins and they would seek the living God and no longer seek answers from the stars. Please Lord Jesus take the blinders off of these people and help them see You, Lord Jesus Christ. Please Lord Jesus I pray that people who are lost and blind have an encounter with You, in Jesus Christ's name I ask these things. Amen

# Breaking Atheism

My Father in Heaven please help those that claim to be into Atheism to see that You are the true and almighty living God. Please loving Father help people to see that You are who You say You are. Father please touch all these people and help them experience your loving hand, here are the names of those that don't believe that I know, now write down on a separate piece of paper all those that aren't saved and pray this prayer.

In Jesus Christ's name I bind up the demonic spirits that keep this person in bondage from receiving the power and knowledge and proof that God is real and He really loves them, in Jesus Christ's name I pray. Amen.

# Binding Attendant Spirits

In Jesus Christ's name I bind up all attendant spirits and I come against you in Jesus Christ's name and I come against the plans you have and I speak to you right now in the name of Jesus Christ and I come against your plans and I ask that all your plans will be ripped apart, broken and crushed in Jesus Christ's name. I pray that there will be a fresh new anointing over my life and there would be mighty breakthroughs coming into my life and I would see the manifestations of the blessings of God cover my life. In Jesus Christ's name I ask these prayers and I plead the blood over these prayers. Amen.

# Spirit of Addiction

I come against the spirit of addiction and I ask You, Lord Jesus, please forgive my ancestors, grandparents, parents and/or myself for allowing this spirit to dictate their lives.

Father in Heaven I ask that you will break the power of addiction and let there be liberty from all addictions. Father in Heaven I know you didn't create me to be dependent on anything, so please Lord Jesus I ask you to push back the enemy and help me walk in the power, authority and freedom in Jesus Christ and I ask You Lord Jesus help me walk in Your power and authority. In Jesus name I pray. Amen.

# Breaking Speaking of Curses

Father in Heaven I humbly come before You and I ask You to please forgive me for speaking curses, claiming I was speaking prayers. Father if I am not asking someone to draw closer to You, Your ways, or Your decrees, or I am not speaking life but death I am being used by the enemy to do his evil deeds, so please Father convict not only my heart but the heart of others

when it comes to prayer, if we are not lined up with the word of God we are being used by Satan to do his evil deeds. So please Father in Heaven continually remind me to speak life even if it is an enemy of mine. In Jesus Christ's name I pray. Amen.

Dear heavenly Father, I ask in Jesus Christ's name that the power of the living God shall pierce the magic circles, secret places and expose the watch towers. Please Heavenly Father, I pray that even when someone paints, draws or makes a pentagram in anyway the power and blood of Jesus Christ shall bring down all demonic powers and authorities and the power of the pentagram shall be bound up no matter where it was painted or drawn and casted down and sent back where it came from. Now thank you Lord Jesus Christ for pulling down all strongholds and bringing every evil and wicked thing into captivity and sending them back where they came from. I praise you Lord Jesus Christ for being so awesome and wonderful. Amen.

Now I seal all my prayers in the Blood of the Lamb and in the power of the Holy Ghost.

# Breaking Channels Between Psychics etc

Father in Heaven, I ask right now in Jesus Christ's name that all the channels between psychics and spirits or between mediums and spirits and all channels will be disrupted and not one person in my city or town operating under a satanic gift of channeling will be able to operate. Heavenly Father, that all lines of communication shall become confused and nothing that anyone who is working under evil influence shall be able to operate right now in Jesus Christ's name I pray. Amen.

# Breaking Power of Crystals

Father in Heaven, I ask right now that you would break and crush a person seeing and feeling the energies of a crystal if it is a satanic or an occult ritual, I ask Father please break the powers of a crystal ball of fortune tellers. Please Father in Heaven remove the spirit of control, heaviness and oppression off their lives and give them a heart to know You, In Jesus Christ's mighty name and in His blood I pray. Amen

# Breaking the Python Spirit

In Jesus Christ's name I come against the Python spirit, Father in Heaven bind up the workings of this spirit right now and I demand in the name of Jesus be gone, you have no authority being in this place and you have no right being here, so in Jesus Christ's name I come against you and I rebuke you, be gone now and do not come back in Jesus Christ's name. f Father in Heaven may Your power and authority reign in this place. Awesome God I love you and I praise Your holy name. Amen.

# Breaking all Demonic Spirits

Dear Heavenly Father I humble myself and come against all demonic spirits that are trying to destroy me or my business. God all mighty, in the name of Jesus Christ, I ask that You would break the power of any and all territory spirits or tutelary spirits. I ask Heavenly Father to please forgive my parents, grandparents and my ancestors of all wrong, evil and wicked doings. I ask Heavenly Father that You would break all generational curses and please give me and my children full access to Your blessings, power and authority in Jesus Christ's name.

Father in Heaven I long to know You and my heart cries out to You, so please allow me to encounter a deepness with You and Father may You give me and my children a heart to know You. Amen. And now I plead the Blood of Jesus Christ over my life, mind, ears, being, heart, soul, and finances. Thank you Father in Heaven for allowing me to know You. amen. In Jesus Christ's mighty name I pray. Amen

# Breaking Spirit of Condemnation

I come against the spirit of Condemnation in the name of Jesus Christ, there is no condemnation and I am free, yes as I shout out freedom my chains are being broken and my walls are crashing down. I am so excited about my new life in Christ and I am now walking in the power, authority and love in Christ and I ask please Lord Jesus Christ help me daily to walk in this new life of Freedom. Amen

# Breaking Spirit of Oppression

In Jesus Christ's name I come against the spirit of oppression, you have no legal right to bind up anyone or any place, so right now in Jesus Christ's name I speak life and life more abundantly over this person or business and I ask Father in Heaven tear down all demonic powers and in Jesus Christ's name I ask Father in Heaven to push back the enemy and don't allow the enemy to advance at all anywhere in this person's life or their business. Now Father please let this person or business experience supernatural break through and may Your most Holy name be lifted up, may people shout from the roof tops just how awesome and wonderful their living and loving God is amen. And may the name of Jesus Christ be highly exalted.

# Spirit of Doubt

In Jesus Christ's name I come against the spirit of doubt, offense, disbelief, self-pity, murder, and hopelessness. Father I need Your help, these spirits seem to be surrounding me everywhere and they are consuming me and I ask that You would please help me fight these demonic attacks and help me walk more like Jesus Christ, so I can walk in humility love, compassion, mercy, understanding and faith fullness. I am so deeply sorry Heavenly Father that I am so self-centered and I am constantly thinking about my pains, hurts and who hasn't been there for me. Lord Jesus consume me in Your presence and may You help me learn how to walk and talk more like You. Father in Heaven please give me the mind of Christ and help me to see that there's a dying world on their way to hell that need Your help. So in Jesus Christ's name I ask Lord Jesus transform me into being like You and help me to walk in Your ways and I ask these things in Jesus Christ's name. Amen

# Breaking Freemasonry

Father in Heaven you are the only true God. You are the Creator of Heaven and earth; I come to you in the name of Jesus Christ your Son, I come as a sinner seeking forgiveness and cleansing from all sins committed against you. I renounce all sins from my parents, grandparents and ancestors. I ask You Father to forgive all my ancestors, parents and

Grandparents for the effects of their sins on my children and me. I confess and renounce all of my own sins. I renounce and rebuke Satan and every spiritual power of his affecting my family and me.

I renounce and forsake all involvement in Freemasonry or any other lodge or craft by my ancestor's parents, grandparents and myself. I renounce Baphomet, the Spirit of Antichrist and the curse of the Luciferian doctrine. I renounce the idolatry, blasphemy, secrecy and deception of Masonry at every level. I specifically renounce the love of position, power, the love of money, greed, and the pride. I renounce all the fears that held me, my parents, grandparents or ancestors to Masons or Luciferians.

I renounce every position held in the lodge by any of my ancestors, grandparents or myself. I renounce the calling of any man "Master", for Jesus Christ is my only Master and Lord and He forbids anyone else having that title. I renounce the entrapping of others into Masonry, and observing the helplessness of others during the rituals. I renounce the effects of Masonry passed on to me through any female ancestor who felt distrusted and rejected by her husband as he entered and attended any lodge and refused to tell her of his secret activities.

I renounce the Hoodwink, the blindfold, and its effects on emotions and eyes, including all confusion, fear of the dark, fear of the light, and fear of sudden noises. I renounce the secret word BOAZ and all it means. I renounce the mixing and mingling of truth and error and the blasphemy of this degree of Masonry. I renounce the noose around the neck, the fear of choking and also every spirit causing asthma, hay fever, emphysema or any other breathing difficulty. I renounce the compass point, sword or spear held against the breast, the fear of death by stabbing pain and the fear of heart attack from this degree.

In the name of Jesus Christ I now pray for healing of... (The throat, vocal cords, nasal passages, sinus, bronchial tubes etc.) And for healing of the speech area, and the release of the Word of God to me and through me and my family. I cut off emotional hardness, apathy, indifference, unbelief, and deep anger from my family and me.

In the name of Jesus Christ I pray for the healing of the chest/lung/heart area and also for the healing of my emotions, and ask to be made sensitive to the Holy Spirit of God.

I renounce the Spirit of Death from the blows to the head enacted as ritual murder, the fear of death, false martyrdom, fear of violent gang attack, assault or rape; and the helplessness of this degree. I renounce the falling into the coffin or stretcher involved in the ritual of murder. I renounce the false resurrection of this degree because only Jesus Christ is the Resurrection and the Life! I also renounce the blasphemous kissing of the Bible on a Witchcraft oath. I cut off all spirits of death, witchcraft and deception and in the name of Jesus Christ I pray for the healing of the stomach, gall bladder, womb, liver and any other organs of my body affected by Masonry.

I renounce the claim that the death of Jesus Christ was a 'dire calamity', and also the deliberate mockery and twisting of the Christian doctrine of the Atonement. I renounce the blasphemy and rejection of the deity of Jesus Christ. I cut off all these curses and their effects on my family and me in the name of Jesus Christ, and I pray for healing of the brain, the mind etc.

# Break all Secret Curses

I renounce all the other oaths taken in the rituals of every other degree and the curses involved. I renounce all other lodges and secret societies such as Prince Hall Freemasonry, Mormonism, The Order of Amaranth, Odd fellows, Buffaloes, Druids, Foresters, Orange, Elks, Moose and Eagles Lodges, the Ku Klux Klan, The Grange, the Woodmen of the World, Riders of the Red Robe, the Knights of Pythias, the Mystic Order of the Veiled Prophets of the Enchanted Realm, the Women's Orders of the Eastern Star and of the White Shrine of Jerusalem, The Girls' order of the Daughters of the Eastern Star, the International Orders of Job's Daughters, Daughters of the Night and Mothers of Darkness

I renounce the All-Seeing Third Eye of Freemasonry or Horus in the forehead and its pagan and occult symbolism. I renounce all false communions taken, all mockery of the redemptive work of Jesus Christ on the cross of Calvary, all unbelief, confusion and depression and all worship of Lucifer as God. I renounce and forsake the lie of Freemasonry that man is not sinful, but merely imperfect and so he can redeem himself through good works. I rejoice that the Bible states that I cannot do a single thing to earn my salvation, but that I can only be saved by grace through faith in Jesus Christ and what He accomplished on the Cross of Calvary.

I renounce all fear of insanity, anguish, death wishes, suicide and death in the name of Jesus Christ. Jesus Christ conquered death and He alone holds the keys of death and hell and I rejoice that He holds my life in His hands now. He came to give me life abundantly and eternally, and I believe His promises.

I renounce all anger, hatred, murderous thoughts, revenge, retaliation, spiritual apathy, false religion, all unbelief, especially unbelief in the Holy Bible as God's Word, and all compromise of God's Word. I renounce all spiritual searching into false religions and all striving to please God, I rest in the knowledge that I have found my Lord and Savior Jesus Christ, and that He has found me.

I will burn all objects in my possession which connect me with all lodges and or cultist organizations, including Masonry, Witchcraft and Mormonism and all regalia, aprons, books of rituals, rings and other jewelery. I renounce the effects of these or other objects of Masonry, such as the compass, the square, the noose or the blindfold, have had on me or my family, in Jesus Name

Now dear, Father God, I ask humbly for the blood of Jesus Christ, your Son, to cleanse me from all these sins I have confessed and renounced, to cleanse my spirit, my soul, my mind, my emotions and every part of my body which has been affected by these sins. In Jesus' name. Amen

# Breaking Meditation

Father, in the name of Jesus Christ Your Son, please forgive me for practicing meditation, trying to find peace of inner self when I should have been looking and seeking for Jesus Christ. Forgive me Father for practicing new age and eastern religion concepts; You are the only one that can offer true peace Lord Jesus Christ. There are no other ways to finding God the Father, everyone must seek You Lord Jesus Christ, You truly are the only way. Amen.

# Feeling Abandoned

Father in Heaven please I call upon You now in this dreadful hour, I feel so isolated, abandoned, hopeless, insecure, depressed, lonely and all alone as if no one cares or understands. Please Father I am crying out to You with all my strength to please break this oppression over my life, please every ounce of me is pleading with You, my loving Father to take away this oppression from me. I don't want to be under this oppression for one more second, please Father in Heaven, every part of me is feeling crushed and all I can do is sit and cry, asking why must I endure this one more second, please now Father come to my rescue in Jesus Christ's Holy name and turn my tears and sorrow into praising and shouting just how awesome my loving Father is, in Jesus Christ's name, sealed in the Blood. Amen

# Dealing with Pain

Father in Heaven, so many are looking for a way to cope with all the pain, stress, hurt, loneliness or fearful things happening today. Sexually transmitted diseases amongst people over the age of 50 has gone way up, leaders of churches and pastors leaving the ministry, so many are having an affair, so many are turning to drugs, prescriptions, turning to alcohol, turning to gambling, turning to sex or porn, so many are thinking if I just get into a religious group or join a cult then I will find hope, so many are leaving their spouse, so many are becoming gay, plus so many are now wanting to go to a hypnosis seminar, so many are turning their backs on You Lord Jesus Christ wanting to find joy, peace, an escape. But Lord Jesus there's only hope in You, there's only peace in You, so I am crying out please, yes, my Lord and Savior, please forgive us of our wicked and evil sins. Please Lord Almighty forgive us for our stupidity, ignorance, pride, selfish ambitions, selfish desires and self-centeredness. In Jesus Christ's name I pray for mercy. Amen.

# Drawing pictures of Angels

Father in the name of Jesus Christ forgive us for drawing pictures and painting pictures of lustful, seductive and perverted angels. God Almighty we have left the knowledge that You God, you are a holy and just God full of purity and righteousness. God forgive us for turning something so holy, pure and loving into such perversion and wickedness. In Jesus Christ's name give us a heart for the things of God. Amen.

# Worshiping Angels

Father in Heaven forgive us please for worshiping Angels. God you are the one and only and we should worship only You. God convict our hearts of such evil and give us a heart to know You and to worship You only. I ask Lord, Thy God, to please call each and every one of us to seek and know the heart of God. God forgive me and forgive this nation for turning its back on You. So I ask that this prayer and all my prayers be sealed in the Blood, power, authority in Jesus Christ's name I pray. Amen

# Bind up the Strongman

Jesus teaches us in the Gospel of Mark 3:27 that we have to bind the strongman. So why are so many Christians and so many authors talk about going on a fast to come against the strong man but that is not at all what Christ said we need to do. So in prayers of Spiritual Warfare, we have to bind the strongman, because it's the strongmen who are Satan's generals. The strongmen control the demons .

PRAYERS OF A WARRIOR

1. Psalm 37:1 The spirit of Jealousy:

Controlling the spirits of envy, hate, bitterness, un-forgiveness, vengefulness, anger, violence, rage, and murder

2. Proverbs 12:22 The Lying spirit :


Controlling the spirits of deception, exaggeration, falsehood, guile, false doctrine, false religions, and craftiness.

3. Leviticus 19:31 Familiar spirit :

Controlling the spirits of Witchcraft, voodoo, Santeria, Juju, Satanism, Divination, witches, diviners, soothsayers, Clairvoyants, Mediums, spells, curses, hexes, potions, lotions, powders, dusts, chants, incantations, sacrifices, offerings, covenants, vows, blood, sperm, fingernails, toenails, hair, urination, and all Occult practices.

4. Ephesians 5:5 Spirit of Perversion :

Controlling the spirits of sexual immorality of any type, fornication, lust, adultery, pornography, prostitution, being gay, child porn, being lustful towards mannequin, Incest, rape, and any sexual practice forbidden by the Word of God.

5. Isaiah 61:3 Spirit of Heaviness :

Controlling the spirits of depression, despair, oppression, hopelessness, fatigue, exhaustion, paranoia, anger, fits of rage, torture, being sadistic, cruelty ,hindrances, blocking of your prayers, and all mental illness.

6. Hosea 4:2 Harlotry

Controlling all spirits that compete with God, ambition in the workplace if used to put down others, sports, good looks and beauty including cosmetic surgery, the love of money, material possessions, Trophies, fame, awards, and corruption.

7. Acts 8 :7 Spirit of Infirmity

Controlling the spirits of sickness, suffering, all diseases, cancer, ailments, disability, pain and terminal illness leading to death.

8. Mark 9 :25 Deaf and Dumb spirit

Controlling the spirits of Epilepsy, all fits, convulsions, speech loss, stuttering, going blind, deafness and dumbness.

9. 2 Timothy 1:7 Spirit of Fear :

Controlling the spirits of anxiety, phobias, compulsive behavior patterns, insomnia, terror, anguish, nightmares, mental illnesses, and all fears.

10. Proverbs 16:18-19 Spirit of Pride :

Controlling the spirits of haughtiness, Egos, arrogance, self-righteousness, refusal to listen and all aspects of the Jezebel spirit.

11. John 8:34 Spirit of Bondage :

Controlling the spirits of domination, control, manipulation, addiction of any kind, OCD, all forms of cult and religious mind control, personal control and bullying in relationships, manipulation, guilt trips, and a corrupted core belief system.

12. 1 John 4:3 Spirit of Anti-Christ :

Controlling the spirits of every cult, creed or religion that rejects Jesus as Lord and Saviour and rejects the Holy Trinity and offers false doctrines that oppose the Word of God, comes against the word of God, comes against praising Jesus Christ, comes against true humility, comes against the anointing of God ,comes against the out pouring of the Holy Spirit or and this spirit comes directly under the dark anointing of the authority of Satan . 13. Matthew 5:21-22  Spirit of Murder: So many people fall prey to getting involved in Gangs, occults, or racism, or fall into greed, insecurities, envy, and selfish desires which lead to murder.

# Breaking your Bloodline

I had a dear friends ask me about bloodline curses because several people have raised their children to be Godly but then turn their back on God because of bloodline curses. So today we are going to come against bloodline curses and speak the power of God over our children and grandchildren...... Dear Heavenly Father, I thank You for the blessing of giving me my children and I thank You for being Almighty God. Father please forgive me for any and all sins that I have committed and I ask Lord, Thy God, that any and all demonic sins which I have committed

will be broken from the bloodline to my children in the spirit to where my children and grandchildren will have the DNA of Jesus Christ to where my children and grandchildren will have the bloodline from those great men and women of God who chose to serve You, worship You, honor You and exalted You. Please Lord Thy God break all demonic strongholds from within them through the bloodline because of my sins. Now I ask Lord Thy God that my son _____ and daughter _____ and all my grandchildren Satan nor any principality nor demonic authority shall have any type of hold on them because my children and grandchildren now have Christ's blood running through them in the spirit because they have Jesus Christ's DNA. Now to my children and grandchildren will seek the heart of Christ and they will walk in righteousness daily. Thank You, Lord Thy God, for putting the fear of God in my children and thank You, Lord Jesus Christ for You shedding Your Blood so now after my children and all my grandchildren get saved they all can enter in to the throne room of God in the spirit freely because the curtain has been torn in half and now they can go right to the Father to repent and to fellowship. Thank You, Jesus Christ, my children are now free because the Blood of Christ is over their minds and all of their being and even their finances. Amen.

# Fulfilling your Destiny

Father in Heaven; I come to you today and I ask that You would please forgive me for my sins and I ask that your Holy Spirit would help me fulfill my calling and destiny by shattering, breaking, destroying and sever all walls and doors around me that are being used as a hindrance by the enemy to stop me. I pray, Lord Thy God that your loving Holy Spirit would rip, destroy, shatter and sever all blinders that the enemy is using to stop me from being the warrior I was called to be. I pray, Lord Thy God that through the power , authority and the blood of Christ I would take back everything the enemy has stolen from me , my family, my territory, my home, my income, my lost wages, my lost time, my lost joy, my lost peace, my lost income, my lost blessings, my lost happiness, my lost sleep, my lost health, my lost blessings, my lost hope, my lost prayer time, my lost mind and my lost study time in the word because Satan declared war against me with his demons but I am now taking it all back by force in Jesus Christ's name because I am a child of the most high God, I am more than a conquer, I can do all things through Christ who strengthens me daily. I have been called to do more than Christ did because Jesus said, you will do greater things then I did. I have the mind of Christ, I have the power of Christ, I have the authority of Christ, I have the compassion of Christ and I have the love of Christ working through me daily because I am a living sacrifice because my heart longs for the things of you almighty loving God to where I am no longer desiring the things of this world because I am so in love with you Lord Jesus Christ. Now through Your Blood, Your anointing power, and through Your name, Jesus Christ, I am pushing back the enemy from all around me to where I am walking in a greater anointing and freedom now Praise Jesus Christ ! AMEN and AMEN

# Protection

Dear Heavenly Father, I humble myself and praise Your Holy Name. I ask that the Blood of Jesus Christ would cover me and be my protection. I now surrender all my hopes, dreams, wants and desires to You, Lord Thy God; yes, Lord, every area of my life I surrender all to You. Right now in Jesus Christ's name, I come against all demonic powers and authorities that would hinder me from fulfilling my God-given calling, purpose, and destiny in life, so in Jesus Christ's mighty name, all hindering spirits I bind you up and send you back where you came from. Now, Heavenly Father, I ask that the promises of God and all the blessing of God would be released in my life to where I would actually see the manifestations of God's increase on my life in every area of my life in Jesus Christ's name.

I will only address myself to the only one and true living God and from this day forward all and any evil entanglements I have had with the enemy I now renounce _____ this and I ask, Lord Thy God, that You will forgive me and these sins will be covered by the Blood of Christ to when the enemy tries to tell God what I did, God almighty will only see the Blood of the Lamb. To where the accuser of the brethren will be silenced. Now Satan I command you and all your agents to leave my presence once and for all for good, I am forgiven and my sins are under the Blood of the Lamb. From now on Satan, there is a bloodline separating me from all demonic powers so unless I sin deliberately you have no power over me. I am transformed now in the image of Christ Jesus, sealed in his Blood. amen.

# Breaking Word and Generational Curses

In Jesus Christ's name I decree and declare that from this day forward all word curses and generational curses will all be uprooted and any evil growth in my soul, my mind or heart will be uprooted and seeds of righteousness will be planted in me. I decree and declare that I will live by the fruit of the spirit and not by the works of the flesh. Lord Jesus Christ I pray that you will forgive me for all my sins and iniquities. Now I humbly ask that the power and authority you walked in, Lord Jesus Christ, will be activated in my life to where I can walk in the power and authority of You, Lord Jesus Christ, to where all evil that tries to come near me will be silenced and will not be able to stay near me. Now in Jesus Christ's name when I pray for myself or for others I will see the manifestation of signs and wonders because the Holy Spirit lives in me and I am praying all demonic forces, witches, Satanist, oculist, even those demon possessed, they will not be able to manifest their powers around me because, He who is in me is greater than the spirits who possessed people to do evil or speak curses. Those that try to channel asking for reinforcements from other demons whether it be from a person or a demon I will break their line of communication and their power, I now will cause the enemy to become confused. I declare and decree that from this day forward when Satan asks me to doubt God or His word I will doubt him, and when Satan tells me to walk in fear I declare and decree that from this day forward I will not put fear in demons because I will speak the name of Jesus Christ over my bills, cupboards, cars, property, paycheck, my home, and my bank account through the power and anointing of Jesus Christ name in the spirit. Do I hear Amen and Amen?

# Power Prayer

Right now in Jesus Christ's name I declare and decree that if anyone uses, my picture, hair, blood, clothes, jewelery, driver's license, social security card, or anything else that would try to manipulate me, curse me, put spell on me, vex or hex me, or try to put a lustful spirit or a seductive spirit on me I come against these things in the name which is above every name and I come against you in the mighty name of Jesus Christ and now I ask that the mighty anointing of Jesus Christ will be released on my life to where I will be able to walk in a greater power, a greater authority, a greater love and a greater compassion to where it will no longer be me coming against authorities of the night, principalities and powers but it will be the power of the Holy Spirit in me that will be shattering, breaking, and severing all demonic powers from advancing in my life but also there be a Holy bloodline put around me because I declare and decree that Jesus Christ is not only my Lord and Savior but I am a child of the most high God to where all the blessings Abraham, Isaac, Moses, Noah, Peter, Paul, and Jesus Christ himself walked in, I can walk in because of God's mercy and compassion. So now I can run to the battle knowing that I am putting fear in demons and even the Jezebel spirit and all the other demonic powers will run in fear because I am living in Christ and Christ is living in me to build the kingdom of God. So I am running to the battle knowing that demonic powers will no longer be able to have open communication lines because of my anointing I am breaking all communication between demons. I praise God I am hearing the roar of Judah. Church it's time to get excited because your break through is now.

# Prayer of Protection for Your Children

Dear Heavenly Father, I humbly come to you in Jesus Christ's mighty name because I am not able to be around my children 24 hours a day I know that demonic influences are all around my children and the enemy will try to attack them in their sleep at times, so Lord Thy God I pray there will be a mighty hedge of protection around my children whether they are at school, spending the night at a friend's house, hanging out with friends or while they sleep, I pray you would confuse the enemy like you did for Elijah when his enemy heard chariots so his enemy became fearful. God Almighty let there be a holy ring of fire around my children from the spears of the enemy to where nothing shall harm them and I pray that if any spirit tries to come against my children's self-worth, self-esteem, emotions, or my children's abilities I pray that any and all spirits will see the Blood of Christ over my children's mind, body and spirit. Now, Lord Thy God, I just ask for a double dose of the Holy Ghost to be around my children day and night whether I am with them or not. I pray that a mighty warrior angel will surround each one of my children 24 hours a day. Now I ask these prayers in Jesus Christ's Name sealed in the Blood of Christ and in the anointing power of the Holy Ghost. Amen.

# Prayer for Finances

When a person is going through financial heartache at times it's very difficult to not fall into depression, anxiety, fear, feeling hopeless and feeling like God has abandoned you. Every human being I know has struggled with these questions of why hasn't my financial breakthrough come in yet? Who can you go to when life doesn't make sense and you need a financial miracle? So what is the answer then?

(1) Go into that secret place, Psalm 91:1-7, He who dwells in the secret place of the Most High Shall abide under the shadow of the Almighty. 2 I will say of the Lord, "He is my refuge and my fortress; My God, in Him I will trust." 3 Surely He shall deliver you from the snare of the fowler, And from the perilous pestilence. 4 He shall cover you with His feathers, And

under His wings you shall take refuge; His truth shall be your shield and buckler. 5 You shall not be afraid of the terror by night, Nor of the arrow that flies by day, 6 Nor of the pestilence that walks in darkness, Nor of the destruction that lays waste at noonday. 7 A thousand may fall at your side, And ten thousand at your right hand; But it shall not come near you.

(2) Offer sacrifices of praise, Then when you are, there is Psalm 27:6 And now my head shall be lifted up above my enemies all around me; Therefore I will offer sacrifices of joy in His tabernacle; I will sing, yes, I will sing praises to the Lord. Hebrews 13:15, Therefore by Him let us continually offer the sacrifice of praise to God, that is, the fruit of our lips, giving thanks to His name. Now ask God to forgive you for any and all your sins, then ask God to bless you by speaking the Word of God. Father in Heaven, Your word declares

(3) But seek first God's will for your life, Isaiah 48:17; Thus says the Lord, your Redeemer, The Holy One of Israel:" I am the Lord your God, Who teaches you to profit, Who leads you by the way you should go. Your word declares that You take pleasure in the prosperity of Your servants, those who favor Your righteous cause (Psalm 35:27). I praise God that Your word says if I would seek Your face first You will open up doors and windows of heaven, miracles will take place and I know that you are my God that can be trusted. Matthew 6:33 But seek first the kingdom of God and His righteousness, and all these things shall be added to you.

(4) Start thanking God that He heard your prayers and your break through is on its way.

Thank you, Heavenly Father, for sending me prosperity, Psalm 118:25 Say now, "I pray, O Lord; O Lord, I pray, send now prosperity. Thank You for continuing to bless my soul, Psalm 121:7 The Lord shall preserve you from all evil; He shall preserve your soul. Because You have given me the ability to create wealth (Deut 8:18), and I have purposed in my heart not to give sparingly or begrudgingly, but faithfully, generously and with a cheerful heart, You will not abandon me in my time of need. All grace will come into my life, so that in every situation I will have more than I need, with resources left over to be a blessing to others (2 Cor 9:6-9).Because I have been faithful in this small thing of living to give, You will make me faithful over much and give to me stewardship of the true riches of life

(Luke 16:10-12). No beneficial thing will You withhold from me (Psalm 84:11). In my house will be wealth and riches (Psalm 112:3), and in that day of prosperity I will rejoice and remember Your goodness (Eccles 7:14) Now I pray that Father Your will be done on earth as it is already done in Heaven I pray amen. Please, Father let there be an increase so I can bless others in need, In Jesus Christ's name I pray sealed in the Blood of Christ and in the power of the Holy Spirit. Amen.

Dear Heavenly Father, please forgive this nation for falling into so much deception by channeling, astral projection, crystals, fortune telling, telepathy, clairvoyance, auto writing, telekinesis, Ouija board, Tarot cards, good luck charms, Horny toad, séances, star gazing, word curses, Mirror gazing, fire gazing, communication with the dead, communication with any animals familiar spirits, trying to communicate with any humans spirits through channeling, soul searching, meditation while masturbating, channel inner core sexual dreams, wanting to perform out of the body, black magic, white magic, soul gazing, mind control, witchcraft, four-leaf clover, rabbit's foot, wishbone, blood drinking, ESP., transcendental meditation, hypnosis, mind-altering drugs, yoga, incense, dungeons and dragons, pendulum, palm reading, body reading, eye meditation, eye reading, horoscopes, signs of zodiac, voodoo, Satanism, Racism, magic, levitation, water witching, Tea leaf reading, secret organizations, worship of angels, worship of prayer, worship of sexual organs, worship of sex or sexual parts, worship of statues, worship of cars or homes, wanting to have sex with a very expensive car, desiring to have sex with animal fur to make contact with its spirit, or desiring to have sex with diamonds or crystals to gain access to their supernatural wealth and power. If there was ever an hour to really seek the true heart of Christ this is that hour. So many souls are lost wanting to serve Christ while wanting to have one foot in the world because they have a deep love for something of this world. It is time to decide who will you truly serve, Jesus Christ or the god of this world. The Holy Spirit is shaking the fence what side will you fall on? Please Lord Thy God pour out the fear of the lord on us like rain!!!

# Your Word Becoming Flesh

Dear Heavenly Father, thank You for having Your word become flesh to where Your Son Jesus Christ came to destroy the works of Satan. Thank You, Lord Jesus Christ for choosing to humble yourself and die on a cross for me and calling me with a holy calling to continue to fulfill the work You were doing. Lord Jesus, please give me a heart to seek your face and to know you deeper. Forgive me please Lord Jesus Christ for all my sins and I ask that Your blood would wash me from all the filth of sin so when the Father looks at me He will not see my sin but He will see Your Blood. I pray You will pour out a fresh new anointing over me to where I can walk in a greater anointing, a greater calling, a greater authority and power so I may destroy the works of Satan and help thousands of people be set free. Please Lord Jesus Christ those that are weak in the spirit and really have no place to go to I pray You will open up the floodgates to give them a place to seek help and get advice from. Please Father put a fire in people that will cause people to know they can live in victory. In Jesus Christ's Name. Amen.

# Prayer for Hedge of Protection

Right now in Jesus Christ's Name, I come before you Heavenly Father and I ask that You will put a hedge of protection around my mind subconsciously or consciously to where doorways will be blocked by the blood of Christ. I pray all tactics from the enemy will be blocked because of the blood of Christ. So right now in the name of Jesus Christ I ask for a fresh new anointing to be poured over me today and as I put on the full armor of God I ask there will be a supernatural hedge of protection put around me with a holy fire to where nothing of evil shall be able to come near me. Now I ask Lord Thy God to convict my heart of any and all wrong doings because I don't want to give Satan a foothold to come in and destroy my life. Right now Lord Thy God I pray that You would give me the strength and wisdom to break away from any ungodly soul tie relationships especially those that are abusive relationships, controlling and domestic violent relationships. Please give me a heart to seek Your face and know Your ways and now I ask You will give me the strength to overcome loneliness and insecurities. Lord Thy God I pray that Your presence will consume me and overtake my emotions, thoughts and ideas to where You would draw me in closer to You, to where You would help me fall so much in love with You to where I would be so consumed in You that my desires for a companion will be removed till you bring someone in my life to where I would no longer be looking or searching for the right person. Now Lord Thy God I ask that all emotions and thoughts that are not of You will be bound up and casted down in Jesus Christ' Name. Amen. Now I ask these things in Jesus Christ's Name sealed in the Blood of the Lamb. Amen.

# Prayer for Help

In Jesus Christ name I bind up these spirits and all spirits connected to them. Spirits of poverty, lack, anger, bestiality, depression, pride, lust, destruction, shame, disgrace, rage, perversion, religion, unbelief, doubt, despair, suicide, control, wickedness, envy, confusion, anxiety, fear, greed, selfishness, Rejection, mental illnesses, bondage, cruelty, divination, sorcery, witchcraft, spells,…homo sexuality, hatred, discord, jealousy, sickness, rape, incest, un-forgiveness, new age, Satanism, occults, murder, failing, torment, idolatry, hopelessness, frustration, foolishness, wickedness, revenge, addictions, mocking, calloused, twisting the truth, seductive, worry, arguing, strife, suffering, illnesses, oppression, violence, seducing, manipulation, Now I loose the spirit of truth, knowledge, long suffering, kindness, love, peace, joy, faithfulness, goodness, forgiveness, mercy, grace, gentleness, self-control, compassion, tongues of fire, wisdom, hope, restoration, healing, intelligence, power, self-discipline, humility, creativity, loyalty, riches, honor, strength, great favor, blessings, wealth, riches, prosperity, and above all the fear of the lord

# Prayer for a Supernatural Encounter

Dear Heavenly Father I pray for all those that have distorted concepts about you, I pray Lord Thy God that they will all have a supernatural

God encounter with You, Father, to help them to come to a deeper understanding of You, Lord Thy God, to where Your love, Your kindness, Your compassion, Your favor and Your forgiveness will be revealed to them, to where Lord only those who choose on their own behalf who choose to reject You shall be lost but all those who open their hearts to You, Lord Thy God, will be openly received because they will know the truth. So thank You and praise You, Lord Thy God, for all that you have done in my life and thank You above all for Your forgiveness and compassion towards me. Lord Thy God; so many witches, Satanists occultists, psychics, mediums, witchdoctors, racist, drug addicts, alcoholics, porn addicts, those deep in to Ouija boards, deep into porn, those that are hoarders, those that work for adult call centers, workaholics and sever sex addicts are all trying to fill that void of trying to find peace, love, and joy because they have all been deceived not knowing You, Father, or Your character, so please Lord Jesus rip the val , smash and severe all demonic hindrances from the enemy trying to stop them from knowing Your character and the Father as well. I pray for an earth shaking, demonic power breaking anointing and a release of a greater anointing to be released to where these people will be able to have a spiritual shattering experience to where no one will have to pray over them because they will each have a Christ encounter to where their chains will be shattered to where addictions, hopelessness, fear, anxiety, torment, hate, and self-pity will be broken off of them in Jesus Christ's name I pray, sealed in the Blood. Amen.

# ADHD Prayer

Dear Heavenly Father, I come before You, asking You to please heal and restore my child. Lord Thy God, Your word says, You did not give us a spirit of fear but of power, love and a sound mind. I am humbling myself and asking you to please restore and heal my child. Demonic powers have come against my child and now they are suffering from _____, and _____ so, Lord Thy God Your word says we can have the mind of Christ so, I ask Lord thy God that You would give me a deep revelation on how to do warfare for my child and do I need to repent or break any generation curses or sins off of my life. Lord thy God you raised the dead through the power of the Holy Spirit so I know you can restore and heal anyone So, please Lord Thy God let there be a shaking in the spirit to where my child will not only have a sound mind but my child will have the mind of Christ and I ask Lord Thy God, You will give my child a testimony and a heart to seek Your face. Lord Thy God, while everyone doubted and ridiculed Jesus when He said the child is not dead, so many laughed and mocked Jesus but, Jesus caused the child to be raised from the dead. Now I ask Father that You would give me a greater faith to where I will be walking, speaking and living in a double portion of the anointing of God to where all doubts, fears, worries, thoughts, and concerns will be casted down to where my faith will not be shaken or moved because of Your great name, Lord Thy God because you are the Great I Am, so Lord Thy God let the heavens be shaken and let all of heaven and earth rejoice because of Your great name, power, authority, compassion, forgiveness and love because my child is healed and set free from all demonic powers, authorities and hindrances in Jesus Christ's name sealed in the Blood of Christ, and through the great Name of Jesus Christ's name which is above every name. Amen and Amen.

# Prayer for Debt

Father in Heaven I come before you and I need your help, I am drowning in debt and I am being overtaken by debt. God Almighty; I ask that you will convict me of any and all sins I have committed especially with finances but, please Lord Thy God don't turn a deaf ear to me but hear my cry for your help. I know Lord Thy God I need to learn to be a better Stuart with money so please Lord Thy God I ask that your Holy Spirit will teach me how to use money wisely and how to be a good Stuart with all and any blessings You have given me. I do realize Lord that all things belong to you so please help me to become mature with my finances and with all my blessings, you have given me. Lord Thy God I know you take pleasure in my prosperity and I know Lord Thy God You want your people to prosper not for selfish gain but so Your people can help those in need with groceries, debts, bills and needs. I realize Lord Thy God I have made mistakes but you are a God that is full of mercy, compassion, forgiveness and grace so even though I have made mistakes I am asking for Your help and guidance because Lord Thy God my heart is being consumed in sorrow and helplessness. So please Lord Thy God I pray that all and any demonic hindrances or sin that is in my life, its power will be broken and Your Holy Spirit will speak to my heart of what I need to repent of. I pray Lord Thy God that if there are any ungodly soul ties in my life that are linked to poverty, lack, rebellion or sin You would deeply convict my heart to where Lord Thy God You will lead me to repentance. So please Lord Thy God give me a heart to seek Your face, to know Your ways and decrees so Lord Thy God I can walk in Your blessings and walk in all of Your promises. I praise you God that all of Your promises are yes and amen. So please give me creative ways, divine favor, divine appointments, supernatural financial breakthroughs, debts paid, people paying me back, supernatural blessings coming in my life, money found, inheritance, money given to me and unknown refunds coming into my life in Jesus Christ name I pray amen.

# Prayer for Pride

Dear Heavenly Father please forgive me for my pride and self-centeredness when I know that Christ is supposed to be the center of my life I have made my needs and wants superior as if I am a god. Father I know the word says to first seek the kingdom of God but so many times I have my wants, my needs, above the kingdom of God to where my emotional, mental, physical, sexual, and comfort needs were more important than seeking You, Heavenly Father, so please Heavenly Father help me mature in the things of the spirit to where I will become that man or woman of God you called me to be so please I ask that all demonic hindrances, powers, and authorities will be blocked and stopped from fulfilling my God given destiny and purpose to where Lord Thy God when I am weak I pray I will be mighty through you Jesus Christ. Heavenly Father I pray that you will increase my wisdom and knowledge to where no matter what area I have been weak in You will give me a greater anointing breaking power to stop me from falling into temptation because I want my heart and focus to be on the things of Your Kingdom Heavenly Father. I pray that when the enemy walks near me like he does so well being a roaring lion I pray his enticing and deceptive words will not cause me to become deceived like he did with Eve to where she took the time to listen, so please Father if it is not You speaking I pray You will train my ears to only listen to You and I pray You will train my eyes to only look to You so I do not fall into deception or trickery. Please Heavenly Father give me a heart to want to seek Your face and know the things of You. I ask that my heart, soul and mind would be transformed by the power of God to want to know the deep things of the spirit through the workings of the Holy Spirit, in Jesus Christ's name I pray through the Blood of Christ and through Jesus Christ name's I pray. Amen and Amen.

Dear Heavenly Father, I pray right now in Jesus Christ's name that through the power and in the anointing of Jesus Christ's name and through the anointing of the Holy Spirit You would bless and touch each and every one of these people because of these people I have developed a stronger prayer life, walk in greater faith, learned to trust Jesus Christ in greater ways, I have been blessed with a greater discernment, learned to press on when everything in me said quit, I have learned to be more bold, I have learned to love those that claim they want to hurt me or kill me, I have learned to love those that ignore me when I let them know I am in need on social media that claimed how they just love me and my ministry but ignored messages sent to just them personally, cried tears that produced an abundant harvest, learned the blessing of planting seeds in the midst of a storm, learned to love God haters even more. Yes, Father I praise Jesus Christ for exposing the hearts of so many and showing me that when people say I love you they mean nothing. So please Lord Thy God I pray for Godly sorrow to come in and touch each and every one of their lives. For Godly sorrow produces repentance so please touch each one of these people in Jesus Christ's name I pray Amen.

*Liars

*Talebearer

*Accuser

*Hater

*Backbiter

*gossiper

*Conspirator

*Betrayer

*Fake Friends

*Fault Finder

*Critic

*Satanist

*mocker

*Schemer

*Warlock

*Witch

*Slanderer

*Doubter

*Two Faced

*Deceiver

*Occultist

*phony

*Religious

*Back-stabbers

*Those trying to put spells, vexes, hexes, or curses on me

*Those trying to put word curses on me

# Directing My Steps

Father in Heaven; I thank you for directing my steps to walk in Your righteousness, blessings, power, authority, love, compassion, forgiveness, and protection. Thank You for being my strong tower, for being my loving friend, being my loving Father, being the parent that I have never had, thank you for covering me with your mighty shadow to where no evil, wickedness, demonic entities, demonic powers or demonic authorities can come near me. I declare and decree that no evil shall be able to come near my dwelling, my family, my home, my property, my work, my body, or my mind. I rebuke right now in Jesus Christ's name any and all demonic hindrances that are trying to stop, block or hinder any of my blessings that are coming my way. I ask Lord Thy God that no demonic strategies, storms, offenses, evil reports or lying tongues will be able to interrupt the blessings of God in my life in any way at all. I ask Lord Thy God there will be a supernatural release of wisdom, knowledge, understanding, power, authority, love and compassion that would be released in my heart to do greater things for Your Kingdom, Lord Jesus Christ, to fulfill my destiny and my purpose to do greater things than You, Jesus Christ, for Your glory and Your kingdom. I also ask, Lord Thy God you would increase my territory to where my tent pegs will be pulled up and I would have a much greater area to where I would see my increase in a mighty way. As my increase of responsibility begins to take place in my life I ask Lord Thy God there will be a shifting in the spirit to where a supernatural financial increase would come and over take me because You have called me to greater things to do for Your glory, Lord Jesus Christ. I pray that the very breath of God will be over my life and Jesus Christ I pray that You would become so tangible to me to where I can feel your very presence. Now I ask lord Thy God that your will be done in my life. Sealed and I will be hidden in Christ Jesus I pray. Amen.

# Breaking Generational Curses

Right now in Jesus Christ's name I confess and proclaim that You are my Lord and Savior over my life, Jesus. I proclaim that through your stripes You bore on the Cross at Calvary, all my sicknesses, diseases and curses are broken. You are my Shepherd, my Healer, my Rock and my Deliverer. I thank You and praise You for being my strong tower, my deliver, my healer, my anchor, my helper and my comforter. I praise Your Holy Name and I praise You, that You are the Great I Am. I break and release myself from all generational curses and iniquities as a result of the sins of my ancestors, grandparents, or parents in the name of Jesus Christ. Lord Jesus Christ, You deserve all praise, all honor, all glory, and, yes, You are the only one that deserves to be exalted and glorified at all times. I am filled with excitement and joy knowing that through Your precious Blood, Lord Jesus Christ I can proclaim these promises over my life because I am free to dance, sing, shout, and know that I am blessed. I am redeemed from the curse through the Blood of Jesus (Galatians 3:13). I am the seed of Abraham, and his blessing is mine (Galatians 3:14). I break and release myself from all generational curses and iniquities as a result of the sins of my ancestors in the name of Jesus. I now declare and decree, I now release myself from all generational curses through the Blood of the Lamb. I break all curses of witchcraft, sorcery, black magic, voodoo, channeling, familiar spirits, perversion and divination curses in the name of Jesus. I break and release myself from all curses of pride, being a bully, or bulling, control, intimidation and rebellion in the name of Jesus. I break and rebuke all curses of sicknesses, diseases, arthritis, weak back, weak joints, weak knees, weak hands, weak arms, weak feet, blindness, deafness, and infirmity in the name of Jesus. I break and release myself from all curses of poverty, lack, being needy, and debt in the name of Jesus. I break and release myself from all curses of rejection, hopelessness, loneliness, depression, anxiety, anger, double-mindedness, fear, stupidity, needing attention, can't concentrate, can't be still, anxious and mental illness in the name of Jesus. Now Father in Heaven; draw me in and give me a heart to know the depths of Jesus Christ heart. Amen and Amen.

# SPIRITUAL WARFARE SCRIPTURES

## Exodus 14:14

The Lord will fight for you, and you shall hold your peace."

## Exodus 23:27-28

"I will send My fear before you, I will cause confusion among all the people to whom you come, and will make all your enemies turn their backs to you. 28 And I will send hornets before you, which shall drive out the Hivite, the Canaanite, and the Hittite from before you.

## Leviticus 19:31

Give no regard to mediums and familiar spirits; do not seek after them, to be defiled by them: I am the Lord your God.

## Joshua 1:9

Have I not commanded you? Be strong and of good courage; do not be afraid, nor be dismayed, for the Lord your God is with you wherever you go

## 1 Kings 18:28

So they cried aloud, and cut themselves, as was their custom, with knives and lances, until the blood gushed out on them.

## 2 Kings 15:16

Then from Tirzah, Menahem attacked Tiphsah, all who were there, and its territory. Because they did not surrender, therefore he attacked it. All the women there who were with child he ripped open.

## Psalm 107:14

He brought them out of darkness and the shadow of death, And broke their chains in pieces.

## Isaiah 40:31

But those who wait on the Lord Shall renew their strength; They shall mount up with wings like eagles, They shall run and not be weary, They shall walk and not faint.

## Jeremiah 24:7

Then I will give them a heart to know Me, that I am the Lord; and they shall be My people, and I will be their God, for they shall return to Me with their whole heart

## Matthew 11:12

And from the days of John the Baptist until now the kingdom of heaven suffers violence, and the violent take it by force.

## Ezekiel 22:30

So I sought for a man among them who would make a wall, and stand in the gap before Me on behalf of the land, that I should not destroy it; but I found no one

## Luke 5:5

But Simon answered and said to Him, "Master, we have toiled all night and caught nothing; nevertheless at Your word I will let down the net."

## Luke 6:46

"But why do you call Me 'Lord, Lord,' and not do the things which I say?

## John 10:10

The thief does not come except to steal, and to kill, and to destroy. I have come that they may have life, and that they may have it more abundantly.

## John 12:32

And I, if I am lifted up from the earth, will draw all peoples to Myself."

## Acts 5:16

Also a multitude gathered from the surrounding cities to Jerusalem, bringing sick people and those who were tormented by unclean spirits, and they were all healed.

## Acts 16:17-18

This girl followed Paul and us, and cried out, saying, "These men are the servants of the Most High God, who proclaim to us the way of salvation."

18 And this she did for many days. But Paul, greatly annoyed, turned and said to the spirit, "I command you in the name of Jesus Christ to come out of her." And he came out that very hour.

## Romans 8:1

There is therefore now no condemnation to those who are in Christ Jesus,[a] who do not walk according to the flesh, but according to the Spirit

## Romans 8:37

Yet in all these things we are more than conquerors through Him who loved us.

# Ephesians 3:14-20

For this reason I bow my knees to the Father of our Lord Jesus Christ,[a]

15 from whom the whole family in heaven and earth is named,

16 that He would grant you, according to the riches of His glory, to be strengthened with might through His Spirit in the inner man,

17 that Christ may dwell in your hearts through faith; that you, being rooted and grounded in love,

18 may be able to comprehend with all the saints what is the width and length and depth and height.

19 to know the love of Christ which passes knowledge; that you may be filled with all the fullness of God.

20 Now to Him who is able to do exceedingly abundantly above all that we ask or think, according to the power that works in us

# Mark 8:17

But Jesus, being aware of it, said to them, (Why do you reason) because you have no bread? Do you not yet perceive nor understand? Is your heart still hardened

# Philippians 2:9

Therefore God also has highly exalted Him and given Him the name which is above every name,

## Philippians 4:13

I can do all things through Christ who strengthens me

## Colossians 1:13-14

He has delivered us from the power of darkness and conveyed us into the kingdom of the Son of His love, 14 in whom we have redemption through His blood, the forgiveness of sins.

## Colossians 2:15

Having disarmed principalities and powers, He made a public spectacle of them, triumphing over them in it.

## 2 Corinthians 5:17

Therefore, if anyone is in Christ, he is a new creation; old things have passed away; behold, all things have become new.

## 2 Corinthians 11:3-4

But I fear, lest somehow, as the serpent deceived Eve by his craftiness, so your minds may be corrupted from the simplicity that is in Christ.

4 For if he who comes preaches another Jesus whom we have not preached, or if you receive a different spirit which you have not received, or a different gospel which you have not accepted—you may well put up with it!

## 2 Corinthians 11:14

And no wonder! For Satan himself transforms himself into an angel of light.

## 1 Timothy 4:1

Now the Spirit expressly says that in latter times some will depart from the faith, giving heed to deceiving spirits and doctrines of demons

## 2 Timothy 1:7

For God has not given us a spirit of fear, but of power and of love and of a sound mind.

## 2 Timothy 3:1-7

But know this, that in the last days perilous times will come:

2 For men will be lovers of themselves, lovers of money, boasters, proud, blasphemers, disobedient to parents, unthankful, unholy,

3 unloving, unforgiving, slanderers, without self-control, brutal, despisers of good,

4 traitors, headstrong, haughty, lovers of pleasure rather than lovers of God, 5 having a form of godliness but denying its power. And from such people turn away!

6 For of this sort are those who creep into households and make captives of gullible women loaded down with sins, led away by various lusts,

7 always learning and never able to come to the knowledge of the truth.

## 2 Timothy 4:18

And the Lord will deliver me from every evil work and preserve me for His heavenly kingdom. To Him be glory forever and ever. Amen!

## Titus 1:16

They profess to know God, but in works they deny Him, being abominable, disobedient, and disqualified for every good work.

## Hebrews 11:6

But without faith it is impossible to please Him, for he who comes to God must believe that He is, and that He is a re-warder of those who diligently seek Him.

## James 3:16

For where envy and self-seeking exist, confusion and every evil thing are there.

## James 4:7

Therefore submit to God. Resist the devil and he will flee from you.

## 1 Peter 2:24

who Himself bore our sins in His own body on the tree, that we, having died to sins, might live for righteousness—by whose stripes you were healed.

## 1 John 3:8

He who sins is of the devil, for the devil has sinned from the beginning. For this purpose the Son of God was manifested, that He might destroy the works of the devil.

## Revelation 12:11

And they overcame him by the blood of the Lamb and by the word of their testimony, and they did not love their lives to the death

## Revelation 16:14

For they are spirits of demons, performing signs, which go out to the kings of the earth and[a] of the whole world, to gather them to the battle of that great day of God Almighty.

## Revelation 21:8

But the cowardly, unbelieving, abominable, murderers, sexually immoral, sorcerers, idolaters, and all liars shall have their part in the lake which burns with fire and brimstone, which is the second death."

Printed in Great Britain
by Amazon

34607845R00046